TWO
SEVENTEENTH-CENTURY
PREFACES

EDITED BY
A. K. CROSTON

Richard Whitlock
ZOOTOMIA
1654

and

Nathaniel Fairfax
A
TREATISE
OF THE
BULK AND SELVEDGE
OF THE
WORLD
1674

UNIVERSITY PRESS OF LIVERPOOL
HODDER & STOUGHTON LTD., LONDON
1949

LIVERPOOL REPRINTS
NUMBER 3

GENERAL EDITOR
L. C. MARTIN

PRINTED IN ENGLAND

C. TINLING & CO., LTD., LIVERPOOL, LONDON AND PRESCOT

INTRODUCTION

NEITHER Whitlock's *Zootomia* nor Fairfax's *Treatise of the Bulk and Selvedge of the World* has ever attracted much critical attention. So far as Fairfax is concerned this is perhaps scarcely to be regretted ; few would nowadays want to read his curious work in full. Nevertheless his style is sufficiently individual and amusing to justify the reprinting of a brief extract. And obviously the most suitable passage to choose is the address *To the Reader*, which both explains and exemplifies Fairfax's notions of how English should be written in the invigorating days of the youthful Royal Society. Whitlock has received slightly more attention : an article by Mr. G. Williamson (*P.Q.*, xv, 1936) has ably shown that his work is of considerable importance in relation to the thought of the seventeenth century. Here again, if a brief extract is to be made, the obvious choice is the *Preface*, which most conveniently shows Whitlock's intellectual range, and also gives an explanation and demonstration of his energetic prose. Both prefaces are of some general interest; more particularly they merit reprinting as examples of two significant varieties of seventeenth-century prose style.

Not very much is to be learned of Richard Whitlock's life. He is not given an entry in the *D.N.B.* What we know of him is almost entirely

gained from Wood's *Athenæ Oxonienses*, which tells us
that he was born in London and that he was aged
16 when he became a commoner of Magdalen Hall
in the Michaelmas term of 1632; it is therefore
likely he was born in 1616. He took his B.A. ' four
years after ' matriculation, became a Fellow of All
Souls in 1638 and B.C.L. in 1640. The title-page
of *Zootomia* calls him ' M.D.', but Wood comments
that ' it does not appear in our registers that he was
so ' : the origin of this degree, as Mr. Williamson
suggests, may be explained by the reference to
' *his* Education *in our own and forraign Academies* ' in
Sir John Birkenhead's note in the first impression of
Zootomia. Wood mentions the publication of this
work in 1654 and remarks that it was

> commended to the world by a letter to the author,
> written by Dr. Jasp. Mayne, who saith for art,
> learning, and variety of matter, put into a hand-
> some dress, the author hath exceeded any writer
> in this kind.

Wood's account of the rest of Whitlock's life is as
follows :

> After Mr. Whitlock had run with the times of
> usurpation, he wheel'd about at the restoration of
> King Charles II. took holy orders, and had a
> small parsonage in Kent conferr'd on him by
> archbishop Sheldon, where he finished his course
> about 1672 or after, as I have been informed by
> Mr. Henry Birkhead his contemporary in Alls.
> coll.

Foster's *Alumni Oxonienses* adds the information that the date of Whitlock's matriculation was 23 November, and of his graduating B.A. 16 June 1635, that 1640 was the date when he was 'called doctor of physic' (? a confusion with the B.C.L.), and that his benefices were Stowe, Bucks (1661) and Ashford, Kent (1662). Apart from its copious illustrations of his intellectual interests, *Zootomia* gives no biographical material except the names of several friends : to those already mentioned may be added Martin Lluelyn, the author of *Men-Miracles*. Except for Birkhead, who retained his fellowship by submission to the visitors, all these friends, it will be noted, were staunch royalists ; they do not seem to have objected to Whitlock's 'running with the times'—perhaps they were prepared to ignore such a lapse in so fervent a defender of learning.

Whitlock's book is varied in form and matter and nearly as allusive as Burton. Its predominating note is a firm dislike of intellectual dogmatism, a dislike tempered by an equal desire to defend true learning from ignorant attacks. In all his opinions Whitlock is guided by a combination of scepticism and eclecticism ; writing during a period of turmoil he urges the need

> to *spunge* out prejudicate *Notions*, or *Opinions*, received on any ground, but that *Scientificall Syllogisme*, where *Reason* is the *Major*, and *Experiment* the *Minor* (p. 258).

The true aim of the educated man is

> To be of *Truths Jury*, not *Knight of the Post* to any

> *Opinion*, or *Interest* : this temper *Serenes* the *Soule*
> from *Passion*, cleareth the *Intellectualls, and* re-
> storeth it (in part) to its first, and best *Independency*
> (p. 226).

Such a quotation as the last would serve well as an
epigraph for the whole work, which, in its dislike
of intolerance and its stress on stoical resignation,
derives explicitly from Seneca, Hall, and Browne.
In its main purpose, the defence of true learning,
is to be seen the influence of Montaigne, Charron,
and ' my Lord *Bacon*, so often in this Discourse
mentioned and yet so necessarily ' (pp. 178-9).
Whitlock deplores the evil results of tying the mind
to particular notions or men, and of confusing
antiquity and authority ; he is here on the side of
the Moderns rather than the Ancients, agreeing
with Bacon that the *latest* age is the truest antiquity
and that the advancement of learning is progressive.
But his main plea is for a *balanced* learning, and his
support for the Moderns goes with a determination
to cull profit from all ages.   He may have ' run
with the times ' in some respects, but he takes a
firm stand against any kind of cultural levelling-
down :

> To say truth, though some call their profound
> Ignorances, New Lights, they were better Ana-
> baptised into the Appellation of Extinguishers
> (p. 160).

Whitlock's attitude to prose style, as we might
expect, is not excessively partisan, but on the whole

his leaning is towards the plain style rather than the ornate. In his preface his references to Seneca, Plutarch, Montaigne, Hall, and Cornwallis put him firmly with the anti-Ciceronians : ' Tracts *of a* continued thread *are* tedious *to most* Fancies '; and he declines the ' Nauseating *of a* continued Allegory'. At times indeed his style is as terse as that of Bacon's early essays ; but he is aware of the later Baconian criticism of Seneca and his imitators, and the nature of his reference to Lipsius links him with the ' loose ' rather than with the ' curt ' Senecan style.[1] And when he deals with misconceptions of the proper style for preaching and writing he shows little patience for the excessive simplicity demanded by the ' affectedly Ignorant ' (p. 250), associating Puritan enthusiasm with indecorous demands for ' *Sermons* easie as *familiar talke*, and printed Labours like those Sermons' (p. 252). Whitlock writes, it must be noted, before the simple style had made its mark on Anglican preaching. In some respects he looks forward to the ideas associated with the Royal Society, sharing their Baconian dislike of dogmatic authority, but stylistically he does not show the unqualified support for simplicity found in most of the divines and scientists of the Restoration; nor would his practice, especially his liking at times for numerous parentheses, always meet with later approval.

This note on Whitlock still leaves much

---

[1] See G. Williamson, ' Senecan Style in the Seventeenth Century', *P.Q.*, xv (1936), pp. 338 and 346.

untouched : of considerable interest, for example, is his defence of the arts—drama, music, painting, and poetry. His defence of the first of these is in the Sidney tradition, though Whitlock has fewer reservations to make : the ' *Dramatick* part of *Poetry* [is] inferiour to none for *usefulnesse* ' (p. 472) ; his regard for poetry in general is seen not only in his essay ' *Profane Inspirations* Plea, or Poetry's Preheminence', but also throughout the whole work in his frequent references : English poets mentioned or quoted include Shakespeare, Ben Jonson, Carew, George Herbert, Davenant, and, most frequently, Donne. But enough has been said to illustrate Whitlock's variety of gifts and his dominating qualities of tolerance, eclecticism, and moral earnestness.

If Whitlock looks backwards as well as forwards, showing the effect of many, not always strictly compatible, intellectual forces, Fairfax shows only one influence of importance, that of the ' New Philosophy ' sponsored by ' that *Fellowship* of *Worthies* in *London*, who are now embodied under the name of *Royal*'.

Nathaniel Fairfax appears in the *D.N.B.* He was born 24 July 1637, his father being the ' ejected incumbent of Rumburgh, Suffolk '. Fairfax was educated at Corpus Christi, Cambridge, where he obtained his M.A. in 1661. During the Commonwealth he held the curacy of Willisham, Suffolk, but was ejected in 1662 for refusing to conform. Giving up the Church he turned to medicine, took a Leyden M.D. in 1670, and spent the rest of his life in practice at Woodbridge, Suffolk, dying there 12 June 1690. He was never a Fellow of the Society he so much admired, but he contributed to its *Philosophical Transactions* several papers on such topics as outsize hail-stones and bodies dead of odd diseases ; and it is worth noting that these articles show Fairfax on familiar terms with ' Dr. *Browne* of *Norwich* '. Fairfax's other published work is *A Treatise of the Bulk and Selvedge of the World. Wherein the Greatness, Littleness and Lastingness of Bodies are freely handled,* which appeared in 1674. This work, as I have suggested, is not likely to attract the modern reader except for its style—an attraction, it must be admitted, which is largely that of a curiosity. But the argument of the book is not without significance in relation to the thought of the age. In particular discussions—which frequently, in his own words, ' beset the mind . . . with wrack and night' (p. 143)—Fairfax is concerned to refute, amongst others, Henry More and Samuel Parker, arguing for instance against the former's belief in a boundless universe and against the latter's conception of the soul as co-extended with the body. Here and in many other ways he shows clear Cartesian influence in his desire to distinguish soul and body, God's infinity and our time, God's ' all-fillingness ' and the world's bounded extension ; he constantly stresses the subjection of the world to natural laws and he frequently uses the analogy of the clock-mechanism. Nevertheless his view of the world is typically unclouded : on the one hand he is little interested in *revealed* religion, and on the other he is firmly convinced of the optimistic faith engendered by contemplation of the natural world—which has political as well as religious lessons to offer :

> If the Commonwealth of Bees were but as narrowly searcht into, as it has been curiously endeavour'd, happily it would shame the misadventures of the cryed up Kingdoms amongst the stock of mankind (p. 152).

How much better, he observes in his ' *Epistle Dedica-catory* ', than the ' *late dayes of Blame, and years of Topsie-turvy* ' is the Restoration world with its ' New Philosophy ' which ' *sets the hand a working not a striking, and answers the noise of Talking by the stilness of Doing* '; it is not ' *shelves full of those Books, that have struck fire for the Government of Churches* ' which make Fairfax feel ' *warmly shined upon by the Father of Lights* '—rather it is ' *the reading of* Malpighius *about the hatching of an egg, or Dr.* Grew *about the sprouting of a Bean*'.

In his views on how English should be written and also in his practice Fairfax carries contemporary notions to extremes. The movement towards un-varnished expression associated with the Royal Society goes so far in Fairfax as to confound itself—the ideal of Perspicuity is lost in the distracting oddities of the surface we are supposed to look through. But Fairfax is merely an extreme partisan in a wide-spread movement of which the clearest manifesto is in Sprat's *History of the Royal Society* (1667). Two articles by Mr. R. F. Jones[1] bring together many extracts from Restoration writers associated with the Royal Society, including most of the Anglican divines and such representative poets as Cowley and Dryden ; and it is clear that Fairfax, though carrying things beyond everybody else (except possibly for Parker's suggestion[2] of an Act of Parliament to put down metaphors), shares the dominating feeling of the time—as he does also in his sturdy nationalism. His conviction of the superiority of English over foreign languages may be compared with Sprat's contrast between ' the Chastity, the newnesse, the vigour of many of our English Fancies ' and ' the corrupt, and swelling metaphors wherewith some of our Neighbours, who most admire themselves, do still adorn their books'. Whether Fairfax's style often demonstrates ' chastity ' is doubtful, but it certainly at times attains ' newnesse ' and ' vigour '.

---

[1] ' Science and English Prose Style 1650-1675', *P.M.L.A.*, xlv (1930) ; ' The Attack on Pulpit Eloquence in the Restoration', *J.E.G.P.*, xxx (1931). The former has a brief note on Fairfax, p. 1007.

[2] In his *Discourse of Ecclesiastical Politie* (1670).

Richard Whitlock

ZOOTOMIA

The Preface

The *Preface,* or an *Antidote* for Authors,
against the Poyson *of* Aspes.

Instructions (Courteous *Reader*) that render
the *Designe* and Purpose of the *Work,* may
well be stiled an *Essay* upon the *Author,* and
as it were *Contents,* of *him,* no lesse then the
Book ; and so may well supply the room of a   5
Dedicatory Epistle to some protecting *Emi-*
nence, or of courting *Apologies,* like *forlorne*
hopes first sent out to set *upon* the *Benevolence* of
Readers. That *Acquaintance* of *Readers* with
the *Contents* of the ensuing *Chapter* might insi- 10
nuate a *Candidness,* I am induced to believe, because with *Well-Meaners* even good Meanings
and *Aymes* in *Authours attone* their *Failings.*
Instead of other kindes of *Epistles,* take therefore this *Anatomy* of the *Anatomy,* (the Book it 15
self) by way of a *Preface* ; and so not tied to
the shortness usual of *Epistles* ; it may serve for
an *Essay* on Mens *Publications* of Themselves
by *Writing,* and more especially on mine. I shall
not here trouble thee with the *Burden* of ma- 20
ny *Epistles* to tell thee this *Qualecunque* (*what-*
soever it shall deserve to be called) was *midwived*
into the *Light* by *Importunity* of *Friends,* or
feare of Antedated *Impressions* ; (with such like
Apologies for encreasing the Number of *Scri-* 25

blers

blers) no, it ventured willingly into the *World :*
if it encrease the *trifles* of the *Presse*, I dare excuse it from adding to the *Guilt :* it was rather
destined to save its *Reputation* by crowding in
somewhat *lesse unprofitable, lesse mischievous,* 5
then the *Presse* daily issueth forth in these *Pam-
phleting* Dayes, bringing forth (to say true) litle
else then *Trifles* or *Invectives.* The *Things* I
present are *nove dicta, etsi non nova,* (according
to *Vincentius Lyrinensis*) *Observations* if not 10
quite *new*, yet in a *new dresse ;* and as *new* things
are acceptable, so among them nothing more
than *new clothes.* The *Old Saw, Nil dictum quod
non dictum prius,* proveth all writings to be but
various *Descant* on plainer *Rudiments ;* or if 15
you will, but the *Anagramms*, the *Alphabet*, and
Transposition of mens various *Collections* from
Men or *Books.* Such are the *Materials* of this ;
one *End* whereof was my *rehearsall* in the
School of the world *:* the same that stirred up 20
Juvenal,
         Semper ego Auditor tantum ?——
And what is that *Rehearsall*, but *doing* of *good*
by *Tongue, Life,* or *Pen,* or *all.* I am not deli-
vered from it by either of those two Argu- 25
ments, either the *Number*, or *Excellency* of
Printed Labours.

    1. Not from the *Number ;* that of S. *Chryso-
stome* beareth me out ; which take in Latine,
                               (not

(not its original) as more easie and fashiona-
ble : *A Scribendi Munere Nos Scriptorum copia
non avocet, vigeat potius, & provocet : bonos libros
qui conscribit, Retia Salutis pandit,* let not the
number (saith he) of *books discourage,* but *provoke* 5
our *Writings* ; he that writeth good *books* sprea-
deth *Nets of Salvation.* Cornelius A Lapide
counteth them requisite, ad Dei Magnificentiam,
& plenam Rerum universitatem, *reckoning
them among those works that* glorifie our Hea- 10
venly Father, *and fill the world as* ornamental-
ly, *nay,* usefully *as many other things.*

2. *Then for the* excellence *of books already
writ, or that* Eximium quid Re, sive modo &
Methodo scribendi, *somewhat excellent in* mat- 15
ter, manner, *or* method *of writing (which A
Lapide requireth in Writers) even the feare of
this is lessen'd by that of* Seneca, Qui ante nos
ista moverunt non Domini sed Duces sunt ; pa-
tet omnibus veritas, nondum est occupata; mul- 20
tum ex illa etiam futuris relictum est. *Former
Writers* Lord *it not over our* Endeavours, *but*
lead *them* ; *all* Truth *is not* engrossed, *after*
Ages *shall travell her* Terra incognita, *her un-
discovered parts : Never did* Momus *himselfe* 25
require all should write best. *To those that write*
better *I shall do the curtesie of a* foile ; *from those
that* write worse, receive the curtesie that I do.
I know not but that it is commendable enough to
make

make the same the Cannon *of our writings, the*
Apostle *doth of Actions,* Phil.4.8.   Finally my
brethren whatsoever things are true, whatsoever things are honest, whatsoever things are
just, whatsoever things are pure, whatsoe-   5
ver things are lovely, whatsoever things are
of good report, if there be any vertue, any
praise, think of these things.   *He that* hit-
teth *on either of these writeth* excusably, *if not*
commendably, *though I think it better may be*   10
tearmed a thing more commendable, than to passe
over the Stage *of the* World *as a* Mute, *leaving*
no Testimony *that he* lived (*much lesse lived to*
the end of his Creation) *his* Being *to be* found no
where *but in the* Church-book : *where it may*   15
be, many of the same name make even that but con-
fusedly known.   And if I should own that which
many Writers dissemblingly decline (*and one of*
the best ingenuously owneth) *I mean an* Aime *at a*
good Esteem (*little or much*) *for my* desires *of*   20
doing Posterity good, *it is but ingenuous* Natures
desire.   *The confirmation of my assertion I cannot*
leave out in either Language.

     An erit qui velle recuset   [*Pers. Satyr.*]
Os populi meruisse ? & cedro digna locutus   25
Linquere, nec Scombros metuentia carmina, nec-
                              (thus.
Non ego cum scribo, si forte quid aptius exit,
Laudari metuam; neque enim mihi cornea fibra
    est.   *Which*

Which take in English from that inimitable
Imitator, and Translator Mr. Holliday.

For doth there breath a man that can reject
A generall praise ? and his own lines neglect ?
Lines worth immortall Cedars recompence,   5
Nere fearing new sold Fish, nor Frankincense.
When I my selfe do write, if from my Brain
Doth flow by greatest chance som happy strain,
(For tis by chance) my heart is not so hard,
So horny, as to feare the due Reward   10
Of deserv'd Fame.————————————

How hypocriticall the declination of this Fame
is let Cicero *tell us,* Tuscul. Quæst.1. Quid nostri Philosophi ? in his ipsis libris quos scribunt
de contemnenda Gloria, sua Nomina inscribunt. 15
Our very Philosophers (*saith he*) *that write of*
contemning Fame, *set their Names to their* Books ;
which they would not, if they were such Decli-
ners *of a* Fame *as they pretend.   But it is not onely*
a naturall *desire, but* Canonical *obedience, (as our* 20
Fame *may be subordinate to our makers* Glory)
to that Apocryphall *Text,* Ecclesiasticus 41.12.
Have regard to thy good Name, a good Life is
but for a few daies, but a good Name endureth
for ever. *A* Charge *seconded by that* Canoni- 25
call Injunction *in the above mentioned* place ; If
                                        there

there be any vertue, any praise, &c. *If* Plinies
Counsell may be heard, he will tell us, Tanto magis quicquid est temporis futilis & caduci, si non
datur Factis (nam horum Materia in aliena
manu) certè studiis proseramus : & quatenus 5
nobis denegatur diu vivere, relinquamus ali-
quid quo nos vixisse testemur. *By how much*
(*saith he*) *our short* time *escapeth* Exploits, *let us*
spin *it out in* Studies ; *and since we cannot* live
long, *let us leave some* lasting Testimony *that we* 10
have lived.   *This* why *I write* at all, *now* why *I*
write thus : *I must use* Mountaignes Apology
in his Essay *of* Books ; I make no doubt (saith
he) but I handle many Themes that are farre
better handled in the scattered works of able 15
Writers : But my intent was not to beat my
Brains in the Acquisition even of Knowledge it
self that was too difficult ; *Nor have I* ; *what came*
easily *among* Authors *or* Observations *to my* un-
derstanding ; *what conduceth to* living *or* dying 20
well, *that I* communicate.   *To say true, I finde*
Mountaignes Pallate (*and not quite without*
judgment) *pretty generall among* Readers *of*
most Ages ; *and because his words are very sig-*
nificant, take them in his own language. Je aime 25
en generall les liures, qui usent les sciences, non
ceux qui les dressent. *I love, saith he, books that*
make use of Sciences, *not* compile *them into their*
Geneticall, *or* Analyticall *Parcels*.   Authors (*to*
                                                    say

say true) are more Thumb'd *that are* variously
usefull, *than those* Embodyers *of* Arts *in* Cancellos suæ Methodi, *into the* limits *of their* proper Method : usefull *I confesse they are, but wan-*
ting the Dulce, Pleasure *of* variety, *and conve-*   5
nience of more contracted brevity : *the* paines *of*
reading *them is seldome bestowed on them, especi-*
ally if they swell *into* Tomes *of that* bignesse,
that he that can have no leisure, *dareth not look*
on them, and he that will have none, careth not.   10
I know not, how but as Montaigne *saith of him-*
selfe, Tracts *of a* continued Thread *are* tedious
to most Fancies, *which of it selfe indeed is of that*
desultory *nature, that it is pleased with* Writings
like Irish Bogs, *that it may* leap *from one* variety   15
to another, than tread *any* beaten Path. *Among*
many kindes of writings I finde Plutarchs *most in-*
viting Imitation for the form, *(call them* Discourses, Essayes, *or what you will)* nor behinde
any for matter ; if mixt sometimes with those   20
Mucrones Sermonum, Enlivening Touches *of*
Seneca *full of* smart Fancy, solid sense *and* accurate reason : *such like* Peeces *compiled by able*
Pen-men *out of* Plutarchs fulness *and* Seneca's
quickness, *would undoubtedly fill the mouth of the*   25
most gaping Expectaltee *among* Readers. Seneca's brevity *alone in some things (as* Controversies, &c.) *might make good that* slander *on him,*
that he did frangere Pondera Rerum Minutijs
Verborum, *crumble the* weight *of* Points. *But for*   30
Hints

Hints *of* Descant *he hath dealt with us, I must
confesse, as he saith of another,* Cupiditatem imi-
tandi fecit, spem abstulit. *Their* fiery liveliness
hath enkindled *a* desire *of* imitation, *and their*
accurateness *hath* damped *all* hopes *of* perfor-   5
mance. *And that in this I write not (as the* Age
discourseth) private spirited Opinions, *take
the confirmation of our* english Divine Seneca, Bishop Hall, *who saith, never any* Heathen
writ more Divinely, *never any* Philosopher *more* 10
probably. *For my using these so frequently, I propounded this* end *to my selfe, even to* shame *our*
Christian dulness, *and slow* Proficiency *under
the* Brightness *of our advantagious* Light, *by making us hear the* Symphony *of the outward* Court 15
of Nature *agreeing with the inner* Quire *of* divine Pen-men ; *for what can we be able to say
for our* selves *? neither knowing, nor following our*
divine Light, *so far as some* Heathen *seem to have*
progressed *in both* Knowledge *and* Practise *mo-* 20
rall. Then why for Politicks *I make* Tacitus *my*
Text, *I need give no other reason than this, never
any better cast* Practise *into* Precept, *or made* History Politicks *in fuller and closer* Observations.
To write Controversies, *engages their* Authors *to* 25
the censure of Factions *and* Parties ; *All things
being so now under* dispute, *that they will not
leave us that* Nos nihil scire *out of question (saith*
Seneca) *not allow us to know that we know no-*
thing :

thing : *I chose therefore a way most* comprehensive, *and least* distastfull *to the quarrelsome world, to handle* Observables *according to their* Nature, *or my* liesure ; *some* larger, *some more* contracted *: the* matter *of them, if you will, is somewhat of that* nature, *my Lord* Bacon *calls* Satyra Seria, *a serious* Satyre, *an endeavour harder to forbeare than undertake, saith the* Poet.

Difficile est Satyram non scribere ; nam quis iniquæ
Tam patiens Urbis, tam ferreus, ut teneat se?

Or if you will, they are what he elsewhere calleth Jnteriora Rerum, *Endeavours* (*in the* Observables *of life*) *to discover and detect the more inward deceits of* men *or* things, *and to* strip *them of their* Appearances. *That I on this* Score *tearm it an* Anatomy of the Living by the Dead, *or* of Practicall Errours (*though in the particulars I decline the* Nauseating *of a* continued Allegory) *doth not much mis-represent my* purpose *; while in the* latitude *of my* Discourses (*and according to the* destin'd Bulk *of this* Tract) *I deliver my* Judgment (*made out of the* seriousness *of* others, *or* casualties of my own Observations) *of* mens mis-apprehendings, *or things* Mis-apprehensions, *whereby the* Glitter *of things oft passeth*

seth for Gold, *while some things* enduring touch
(*but* dull *to the eye*) *arise not to an* Esteem *equall
with* counterfeits, *as in nothing more appeares
than our* Opinion *of the* World *and its* Desira-
bles *in grosse, dreaming of* life *in a* Carkass, *and* 5
of Perpetuity *in a* blast ; *and having high* con-
ceits *of our* vain Projects, deare ones *of our* vexations, *and* doting ones *of falsely admired* Con-
temptibles. *But come we to* particulars, *and it is*
undeniable *but that there are in* (*even the most* fa- 10
miliar) Passages *between* man *and* man, *neglect-
ed* (*but on enquiry easily* discoverable) *false* Principles, Erroures *and* causes *of* Miscarriage, *and
in many things* inner parts *unobserved by the
carelesse* world, Errores Vulgi, vulgar Errors 15
reaching to the Morals *of men as well as their* Philosophy ; *the* substance *of these* Discourses *the*
Poet *giveth you most fully.*

Quicquid agunt homines, Votum, Timor, Ira,
　　　　　　　　　　　　　(voluptas, 20
Gaudia, Discursus, Nostri est Farrago libelli.
Et quando uberior vitiorum Copia ?

　　Which take englished from Sir Robert Stapyl-
　　　　tons *ingenuous Translation.*

What men do, their hopes, feares, distasts, 　25
Sports, Fates, the Medly is our Book presents.
And when was sin more fruitfull ? 　　*They*

They are Collections *many of them more from*
men *than* books, *in which latter we seldome meet*
with live, *and particular* presentments *of mens*
Principles *and* Actions ; *indeed* Poets *do it best,*
and among them the Dramatick; *the* form *of* 5
them I owe as little to Books ; *for I must truly*
acknowledge I did not so much as cast my Eye *on*
Books *of the* like nature (*without it were my*
Lord Bacons Interiora Rerum) *till they were*
compiled, *and then chiefly to avoid* Actum agere, 10
writing the same things, at least in the same manner ; *not out of* presumption *of my own* Abilities
to go alone, without their help, *but out of an* Idio-
syncrasis (*or particular* Temper) *of my* Fancy,
(blameable *or* commendable, *I determine not*) 15
to which Imitation *is an unpleasing* Confine-
ment, *and* (*I know not how*) *more laborious than*
Invention. *That some of these are mixt with* Di-
vinity, *the* Title *assureth you* : *nor am I ashamed*
to professe it, since it is without Intrusion *into the* 20
Office *of those* Secretaries of Heaven, *to whom*
are committed the more Mysterious Oracles *of*
our Credenda, Creed ; Errors *of* Faith *I leave*
to those (*sufficient for such things*) *to correct,*
but Errors of life *I know not why we should not* 25
amend *in* each other. *That some of them are not*
onely mixt, *but are* professedly Essayes *in* Di-
vinity, *transgresseth not the* Nature *or* Lawes *of*
this kind of writing in mixt discourses, *and I am*
                                        sure

sure to serious Soules *will not be* unwelcome ;
since all Writings (*as well as* Actions) *are but*
Trifles *in comparison of what* referreth *to* Eter-
nity. *Nor will it be an* Apology *onely, but* (*with
such*) *a* commendation, *to say I propounded that* 5
end Seneca *giveth us in* charge, hæc alijs dic,
ut dum dicis, audias; ipse scribe, ut dum scripse-
ris legas, *Epist*.89. *Give serious advise to others
that thou mayest be thine own Auditor, and write
profitable for thine own perusall. As for being seri-* 10
ous in Discourses *with* Posterity (*such are* Pen-
nings *for the* publike view) *let it seem as mis-
shapen or uncouth as it will to* Antick Fancies ;
I am sure printed vanity *is double unprofitable-
ness* ; *to be* Foole, *or* Knave *in* Print *doth but dou-* 15
ble the Blot. *Usefull* Scripts, *or* Writers Seneca *giveth* (*I am sure*) *a higher* Character *of,
than of many other* things, *or* men ; *that some*
(*which would be counted the* worlds wise ones)
set so high a price on. Si hoc mecum, si hoc cum 20
Posteris loquor, non videor tibi plus prodesse
quam? cum ad vadimonium Advocatus descen-
derem, &c. mihi crede, qui nihil agere videntur
majora agunt; humana, divinaq; simul tractant.
While I discourse (*saith he*) *these things with* 25
my selfe, and Posterity, *do not I profit more than
if I* voted *in the* Senate, *pleaded before a* Judge ?
&c. *believe it, though usefull* Employments *of the*
Pen *may seem idle* Enterprises, *it is far above*
many

many Employments, *falsely* (*if compared*) coun-
ted weighty. *The* youngest *of us I am sure may
say as* Seneca, premit a Tergo Æternitas (etsi non *Senectus*) & obijcit annos inter vana
studia consumptos : tanto magis urgeamus, & 5
Damna Ætatis male exactæ labor resarciat. *E-
ternity* (*though not old Age*) *pulls us by the* Sleeve,
and upbraideth the mis-spending *of our former
yeers in vain and fruitlesse* Studies, *and calls on
us to* redeem *them by some* labours *for the good of* 10
our selves and others. *The whole* Tenor *of this*
Peece *is* perswasion *of others, nor a lesse* obliging
my selfe. *For* Books (Seneca *saith*) *are* Bills of
our Hands *to the* world ; *and indeed I think
them more, being little lesse than* Vowes to God 15
before men, *and to* men promises before God of
a mindfulness *of our* Vow *made in* Baptisme *of*
Renouncing the worlds vanities, *that by nothing
more have got into our* Affections, *than by an* Erroneous Estimate *of the* reall Worth *of things,* 20
or undiscerning the fallacious insides *that appeare
when things are* stript. *If any among these* Observations *seem* Paradoxicall *to* Credulous Igno-
rance (*that swalloweth* Traditions *for* Truthes)
or distastfull *to the* Guilty, *according to* Marti- 25
all.

Ecce rubet quidam, pallet, stupet, oscitat, odit,
Hoc volo ; nunc nobis carmina nostra placent.

At

——————————————At what we say,
One blushes, or looks pale, is ill at ease,
Amaz'd, takes pet ; why now our Verses
  please.

If either of these I say, I have my End ; *one main* 5
end of my writing being (*like* Diogenes *his go-*
ing into the Theater *against the* throng *of* people *coming out*) *to let the* World *know* I think
not *as* shee thinketh, *and yet think never the*
worse *of* my selfe ; Erasmus *assuring me it is* bo- 10
na pars sapientiæ nosse stultas vulgi cupidita-
tes & absurdas Opiniones : *A good* step *in* Pru-
dence *to know and dislike the* foolish desires *and*
absurd Opinions *of the* Vulgar.   *In* controversies
I dissent *without* Peremptoriness *or* uncharita- 15
bleness, *and will* Salve *the deepest* Gashes *of* Detraction, *or* prejudice *against my* boldness *in*
dissenting, *with that* conclusion *of* Servius *his*
book of the weapon salve : Quæ sanctissimi viri
& doctissimi firma rataque sanxerunt, ea solum 20
in nostra Dissertatione firma rataque sunto.
What the Learned *and* Religious *assent to* (*and*
no other) *in our* Writings *shall have so much of*
Obligation *over any mans* assent, *as thereunto* to
stand in full force and vertue.   *As for* Exactness 25
of writing on any Subject *in* Poetick heights *of*
Fancy, *or* Rhetoricall Descants *of* Applicati-
on, *I leave to the* Endeavourers *in both those noble*
                                    Studies

Studies, *whose* profession *it is to spend the* vigor *of their* Conceptions *on a* Theme, *to* speak *as* never any before, *and if possible to* damp *the imitation of* Posterity. *For my own part I may say, as* Lipsius *in his Epistles* ; Rationem meam scribendi scire vis ? fundo, non scribo, nec id nisi in Calore & interno quodam Impetu, haud aliter quam Poetæ. *Would you know (saith he) my manner of writing? it is a kind of voluntary* Tiding of, *not* Pumping for ; Notions flowing, *not* forced ; *like* Poets unconstrained Heats *and* Raptures : *such is* mine, *rather a* running Discourse *than a* Grave-paced Exactnes ; *having in them this* Formality *of* Essayes *(as Sir* W. Cornwallyes *saith of his) that they are* Tryals *of bringing my* hand *and* Fancy acquainted *in this using my* Paper, *as the* Painters Boy *a* Board *he blurs with* Tryals. J *may say in my defence as another before me,* Sicut in magna sylva boni venatoris est Feras quam plurimas indaganter capere, nec cuiquam culpæ fuit non omnes cepisse : *As in Hunting he is the best* Huntsman *that catcheth most, and not* bad *because he* catcheth not all *: To comprehend all, or most can be said on any of these* Themes, *I professe not* ; *no, I feare that of* Ludovicus Vives, *in* attempts ad ultimum Naturæ, *straining our Abilities,* Ingenia supra vires aspirantia infra Mediocritatem subsidunt : *Wits that flye above the* Spheare *of their* Activity, *fall* beneath ordinary

perfor-

performances ; *and were I one of such* Labourers
in vain, *I should never* please *my self, but still be
at his* fault *that could never take* Manum de ta-
bula, *his Hand off, but was still* mending, disliking,
interlining, *& it may be at last* corrected *all with* 5
a Spunge : (*I have much a do to forbeare it now
my selfe*) *it was the fault of* Protogenes (*as*
Apelles *accuseth him*) Qui nimia peccarat di-
ligentiâ, *who offended with too* peevish diligence ;
a fault they blame Paulus Æmilius Veronensis 10
with, of whom it is said, nunquam sibi satisfa-
ciebat, sed quoties sua recognoscebat, diceres o-
pus non correctum, sed aliud. *He never was pleased with his own* work ; *if he went to* correct *it,
you would say it were a* new, *not* reform'd peece : 15
As for my Quotations (*which in the Judgments
of some are dasht* (*like* Pedigrees) *with a* vix ea
nostra voco—*scarce worth being called our own*)
I have on purpose confirmed some of my Descants
(*as well as at first I had them thence* hinted) *from* 20
such able Pens *as are unquestionable.* *All* Writings *are but* Hints, Descant, *or* Confirmation ;
if any be our own, it may well enough satisfie Ex-
pectation *from any* Single (*unlesse singular*) Author. *He is a usefull Servant to* Truth *that ser-* 25
*veth her by either, though not by all. Besides such
is the* peevishnesse of present times, Contempo-
raries *speaking even the words of the* Ancients,
have no Authority, *unlesse they* disown them *by*
                                        Citation

Citation : *my Citations are from that Princi-*
ple of doing as I would be done by, *doing my*
Reader Service *by a* Reference *to some usefull*
Book (or part of it) that may recompence his perusall *of mine. I have my selfe sometimes been more*   5
beholding to some Books *for anothers* Sense, *than*
their own. *The like may befall this. As for my*
declining in many places Grammaticall Transla-
tions, *it is to bring the* Sense *neerer my* Purpose
in our own Idiom ; *and where I do not* translate, 10
(or differently) to my Remembrance *I have en-*
deavoured to continue the Sense, *that the severall*
Languages *need not trouble the* english Reader *so*
much as a Parenthesis. *For the* Pleasantnes *of som*
of these Tell-troths, *let the* world excuse me, *if I* 15
play with my Vexations, *and turn my* Experi-
enc'd Torture *to* Delight, *as knowing no better*
Revenge *on (no nor* Cure *of)* vulgar Stupidity,
(specially in Concernments *of* Physick, *and their*
own Health) *than*——Ridentem dicere verum, 20
to tell them Truths pleasantly, *since it is the con-*
stant humour *of the* people *to love the* Jigg *bet-*
ter, than any good or serious part of the Play. *Last-*
ly for Detraction *and* Censure *(the* Hydra *all*
Authors must encounter) it is more my scorn *than* 25
feare, *and ought to be to any* Venturer *abroad in-*
to publike view ; *or else he may lye open to such*
disheartnings, *as become not the* confidence *requi-*
site to these undertakings. *The rarest* Antidote
(not

(*not onely against the* Venome, *but very* Hissings
of this Hydra) *that I meet with,* I am Debtor *to
our* English Bernard *for, in his Epistle before the
third* Century *of* Meditations, Those thoughts
which our Experience hath found comfortable 5
and fruitfull to our selves, should with neglect
of all censures be communicated to others ; the
concealment whereof (me-thinks) can proceed
from no other ground but Timorousness or
Envy. *Wherefore* Horace *his* Resolution *may be-* 10
come serious *Writers.*

   ——Valeat res ludicra, si me
Palma negata macrum, donata reddit opimum.
    ——I'le ne're write Toyes,
  If I must pine or thrive on th'vulgar Noise. 15
If Authors Carp (*were not my* Principle *of* Cha-
rity *other wise*) *J could* momize *and* cavil *at* Matter *or* Form (*more or lesse I believe*) *of their* Labours : *at my own I am sure I can and do* (*it may be
where they do not*) *yet think not my selfe enslaved* 20
so much to any ones Curiosity, *as to correct and stil
mend, like a* totall Alteration. *If they be not* Authors, *I value not their telling* Bellarmine, *he
lies, when possibility of answer is denied him. As for
any either* Perfunctory Reader, *or too* severe 25
Censurer (*free of the* Company *of* Pish-mon-
gers) *that* Pisheth *at any thing not exact, either
in it selfe, or in compliance with his* Humour ; *I
answer, the* Stationer (*my* Porter) *mistook the*
          deli-

delivery *of the* Letter (*my* Book) *for it was di-
rected onely to the* Candid Interpreter *of* modest
Endeavours, *not* Exacter *of* Impossibles, *or* un-
seemlies ; viz. Perfection *as the one, and to generall* Compliance *as the other. To all* gaping Ex- 5
pectaltees (*that look for more than here they are
like to finde*) *my* Book *replyeth with this its* mot-
to; *not* queint, *but* useful; *or, not* rare but honest,
at least in the Authors Iudgment *and* Intention;
and I will use the words of an Ingenuous Author 10
of our own, being so apt to my purpose *: I like
much better to do well, than talke well, chusing rather to be* beloved *than* admired, *aspiring to no
more height than the comfort of a* good consci-
ence, *and doing good to some, harme to none. If* 15
my Essayes *speak thus, they speak as* I *would have
them. Thus far he, as fit as if he spoke for me of a-
ny thing amongst them.* I *will likewise add what*
Walafridus Strabo de rebus Ecclesiasticis *said.*

Si quid in hoc (Lector) placet, assignare me- 20
                            (mento
Id Domino : quicquid displicet, hocce mihi.

If any thing that's good i' th' Book you see,
Ascribe to God ; but what distasts, to mee.

   I *know there is not any one* Divell *compasseth the* 25
Earth more than that Erasmus *speaketh of :* Adeo
                              nunc

nunc in omnes & omnia, per universum Orbem
grassatur comitata furiis ἡ Διαβολὴ, ut non sit
tutum ullum emittere Librum nisi Satellitio mu-
nitum.   *The* Devil Calumny (*saith he*) *against*
all men, *and* all things, *doth so* rage *in these* dayes,   5
that it is not safe setting out *any thing* unguard-
ed. *If the* integrity *of the* End *may plead for the*
Matter *or* Form *of this Book*, *I may hope* absolu-
tion ; *its chief* Designe *being to* double the guards
of the Negligent, *that suffer* erroneous mis-judg-   10
ings *to* surprize *their* Inadvertency : *or to awaken*
the lazie drousinesse *of others that are loth to be*
rowz'd out of Errors pleasing dream ; *and to*
correct *the* vanity *of* most, *that* spend *their* time
or thoughts *on* impertinencies, besides, *or* below   15
the noble end their souls *were* destined *for*.   *For*
two lengths *I must insert these* short Apologies *:*
the one of some of these following Discourses, *the*
other of this Preface : *the* former *need deterre no*
man, *if he be of* my minde, *with whom the* flat-   20
nesse, *or* sharpnesse *of* an Author, *is in stead of*
Rests.   Indisposednesse *in my* self, *or a* dull *period*
in an Author *maketh me* turn down *the leaf*, (*if*
my businesse *do not*) *as well as any* Division *of*
Sections *or* Chapters, *&c. by much the younger*   25
brothers *of* writing it self, *and even in* sacred
Writ *but of* (*almost*) modern Authority. *Again*,
the nature *of this kinde of writing is like* free
                                              speeches

speeches *in the Parliament of* Parnassus, *or* Liberavi Animams, *whose* length *or* shortnesse *is from
the* Authors sense, *not any* stint *of* Rule, *or* Order.
For the length of the other, (*this* Preface) *it's*
Name *were enough, if we follow the* Allegory *of a*   5
Porch *and* Building,: *I have, I am sure, come
far short of* Solomons proportion *of* twenty *to*
sixty, *as it is observed by that* Secretary *to Wit,
Reverend* Dr. Donne : *or if,* Reader, *thou be in
the* number *of such as account* Epistles, *and* Pre-   10
faces *materiall* part *of a* Book. *And now I am
excusing the* Books Geometry, *give me leave to
excuse its unexpected* bulk, *and thicknesse, from
meer mistake that my writing had not been so* close.
But I write not this, *nor the* Book, *to any* curious   15
in the shapes & outsides *of* Books, *or that think it
necessary to a* Books *handsomnesse,* (*as well as* wo-
mans) *to be* slender in the waste; *but it is now past
cure, and must venture abroad with all its* faults,
materiall, *or in* printing; *which may be more then*   20
should, by reason of my distance from the Presse.
Some principall Errata's *are* mentioned ; *the rest,
an* ordinary English *Critique may correct in his*
reading. *I shall therefore conclude with letting
thee know, what* Reader *I* slight, *and what I* ho-   25
nour, *in the words of* Erasmus, *in his* Enchiridion
Militis Christiani :

Nil

Nil moror aut laudes, levis aut convitia vulgi *:*
Pulchrum est vel doctis, vel placuisse Piis :
Spe quoq; majus erit, mihi si contingat utrumq;

> *The flouts or th' praise o'th' vulgar I not weigh,*
> *If Learn'd or Pious men content I may :*   5
> *But O ! if both, a Joy unhop'd 't would be.*

> > *The* good, *and* good will *of thee* (*if thou*
> > *be either of these*) *is the* Desire *and*
> > Endeavour *of*

Thy true honourer,   10

R. W.

Nathaniel Fairfax

A
Treatise
of the
Bulk and Selvedge
of the
World

To the Reader

F I may measure others by my self, 'tis a more ticklish thing to pen a Preface, than 'tis to write a Book. For when ever I lay hands on a New 5 piece, as soon as I have once spell'd the Great letters of its Name, I am wont hastily to take forth to the Fore-speech for the Reader, as thinking that to be the handle, that I am to hold the Book 10 by, which, according as I relish or mislike, oftentimes so fares the whole with me. For if I find the man has it not in him to erect a Scheme in the *Say* that he has for me there, I am shrewdly given to mistrust, that he will 15 never conjure much in the Book that comes after : or when the first Greeting me is sowre or faint, I am ready to fear the after treat will be none of the sweetest or the win-ningest. Whether others conne Books with 20 these kind of reckonings, I can't tell ; but while I can tell my self that I do so, it stands me in hand to be a little wary of trip-ping upon such slippery ground. Now to speak truth, all the tale that I have to tell 25 the Reader is but this : That finding in my self a kind of forwardness towards Philoso-phy, and mainly to that part of it which

takes

takes knowledge of Bodies ; as which, of all
others, I found I could receive most helps
and furtherance in, from those spreading
lights and wealthy stores, with which the
Royal Society at home and others abroad, 5
set into the way by their showing and en-
heartned to go on by their works, had
both embellisht and enricht it, I let my
mind alone to take its full swing in the
Conning of Bodies, this and that ; and forth- 10
with or ere I could well help it, I fell a
Roving, and plung'd out from what I was
medling with and tossing of, to another
thing that was earlyer and Bulkier, and to
somwhat still that was more betimes and 15
more of Boak ; and being quite lost in a
wilde and a frightful on and on, I e'en took
back again where I was, and fell to unra-
vel the thing that was too big to be fa-
thom'd, that I might make it little enough 20
for my mind to grapple with : but I was as
unluckie at lessening and narrowing as I
had been before at widening and big-
ning. As the one had wrackt and limm'd
my thoughts, with endless tenters and 25
boundless retchings out ; so had the other
nipt in my soul and shrivell'd up my
thoughts, with restless gripes and unwearyed
parings off : so that I had both lost and be-
nothing'd my self in the lessenings made
within

within my self, as I had lost and bewildred
my self in the scopes still left without my
self. Nor could I be at rest in my mind, till I
had tryed, whether I could not cut off Boundlessness and endlessness, so as at length I 5
might have ease, to find, that *Body*, which I
had to do withal, had both beginning and
end, an inmost part and an outmost whole,
as I my self had : and so the remarks and ex-
periments that I was to make, were not up- 10
on Bodies that carried Boundlessness in their
bellies, & were themselves a swimming in a
boundless gulf, so that I must needs have my
thoughts to dance after them in an endless
round, or launch into a boundless width ; 15
but that I might settle here or pitch down
there, and tell the first and ken the last, and
cope with the *biggest* and the *least :* and as
soon as I got to the spring head of *Lastingness,* I sate me down and drank a health to 20
sweet rest, and blisst my self that I was
there ; and when I came at the *Selvedge* of
Bulk, I took heart afresh to think with my
self, that there was all, and nothing at all
beyond, and I need weary my self with no 25
more wandrings in a wast, but might come
home again fair and soft, and fasten on this
or that, or little or great, as I thought best,
to set a mark on or make a Tryal of. For
then I saw that all was not wood within a
wood,

wood : but me-thought the world was a curious Frame of well set Bodies, the *beginning* of
which, the *least* of which, and the *whole* of
which, might all be come at.

Thus having shaken off the things I could 5
never grasp, and taken Body by the right handle, I found I was freer to think, and better
at ease to work : and deeming there were
more in the world that were of my *make*, I
did not know but they might think, and do 10
so too ; and it was but a friendly part to set
any man into his way, that I thought was out
of it : and therefore what I thought I writ, and
what I writ, the Reader sees is comen abroad.

Which if it takes, I shall not mislike it, that 15
another man has found that which he lookt
for ; and if it does not, the worst on't is but
this, that that which has not yet been made
out by any man, nor has it been by me. And
whatever ill luck betides it, I have no body 20
else to blame for it ; for I writ it all at home,
and 'twas given at my self. And to tell troth, I
don't love to ask another man, whether my
Child be not pretty or hopeful ; for I think,
that must needs be a crotchet piece of un- 25
luckyness, that is not fit to be Printed if a
friend has it to read over for that end, or
to be prais'd, if another man has it to make a
New song upon.

But if any man ask me what I think on't my
self ?

self? I answer, The very same that I think of o-
ther mens writings, and that is, that they are
the writings of Man and nothing more, writing and miswriting mingled together. Only
I can say the Writer indeed is neither Green 5
nor Grey. So though the Reader may fear he
shall find little that is full ripe, I hope he will
find less that is altogether raw. As I think o-
therwise from what I did some years agoe, so
happily I may think otherwise from what I 10
do some years hence, even about some things
here spoken to : and therefore I love to speak
soft for my own sake as well as others. I do believe too if I had kept it longer I could have
drawn it up better, but that bare no sway 15
with me to do so ; for then the only day of its
coming into the world must have been the
day of my going out of it. Notwithstanding
though I don't believe 'tis the best that can
be done, or the best that I could do my self, 20
yet 'tis rid of as many mislikes as I could
strike out at twice reading, and I did not
think it worth while to read it again to find
more. As 'tis, I neither reckon it my God nor
my Golden Calf, nor am I fond on't or a- 25
shamd on't. Should I say I had slighty thoughts
of it, I can't tell how it would be wit or good
manners to put it into the hands of my
Betters ; and if I give out I set highly by
it, I should lacken it as much by making
                                                   such

such a Fondling the Penman of it.   However
the management of it may seem weak or
low, I am sure the drift and scope was manly
& lofty.   There being no lower nor other aims
in it, than that we might not think amiss of 5
that Almighty Being which has made us, nor
of the sundry Beings he has made, that we
may neither dote nor dare, stragle nor be lost :
but may be led by such a clue of understand-
ing, & softned by such a bashfulness of know- 10
ledge, that we may be wise and awful both in
one ; that the knowledg of things may be less a
weariness to the flesh, and that thoughts of
things without us may less gall that Being
within us ; that, as God beholding what he had 15
made, said with himself that all was good, we
may see it & say it too, & love the spring from
whence they came, while we wonder at the
wisdom by which they are ; worshipping the
same with a more becoming dread, a fuller 20
enlightned mind, freer out-goings of heart,
steddyer & closer thoughts about things that
he has made more easeful to the mind, and
better sorted in it : that so giving to God his
right, we may take to our selves our own rest. 25
   In the doing of which, the freedom that I
have taken, I give too.   *Think and let think*,
are engraven upon my very soul.   And I shall
never think amiss of the Reader for not being
of my mind, any more than I do of those
                                          Learned

Learned men which I thought meet somwhere
to name. Which I did, not from any itching to
thwart them : but I thought it would speak nothing of Breeding, to look full on a Great man
standing in my way, and not to vouchsafe him 5
worth Doffing to, or to write my self of another
mind from what some men of Name are, whose
reasons for what they hold have fallen into a
many good hands, without I should also say why
I am not of their mind for their reason. But as 10
for any lessenings of them, who have done huge
well, as I think, elsewhere, and may have done
well enough, as others think, where I take them
to be out ; 'tis so much against my meaning
and the very Grain of me to let any such fall 15
from my Pen, that if in any thing I so much as
but seem to do it, 'tis all my unwariness, and nothing of my aim. And I do think my self so
much the more bound to take heed how I handle the good name of others, by how much the 20
more I see, how an ill will'd and frampled was-
pishness has broken forth, to the royling and fi-
ring of the age wherein we live, and for ought I
can foretel, even those too, that are coming after.

Indeed, when I read such things as are spoken 25
to, further on, in a late Writer, I can't for my life
but think, *he* may mistake a little, as you and I
and all men do, and have done & shall do. And
that thereupon he would not willingly be call'd
Names, such as can't be spoken without a stinking

ing breath, nor written but with a brazen pen,
nor spell'd but with the letters of the Dog and
the Goose, the grinning and the hissing. And re-
membring 'tis good Bible, *Do as you would be
done by*, I can easily let go my self in some for- 5
ward wishes leading to self love in behalf of such
a one, heartily bespeaking him, for Gods sake,
for that of *self*, & the Commonwealth of Learning, that hereafter we might read writings with
other sentences besides those of Condemnation, 10
with other wit besides that which lies in the
forehead, and where all the Dashes of the pen
may not be stroaks upon men ; as knowing that
such *Doomesday Books*, may soonest be burnt
themselves, which are readiest to enflame others. 15

I believe no man wishes with more earnestness
than I do, that all men of Learning and knowledg were men of kindness and sweetness, & that
such as can outdo others would outlove them
too; especially while *self* bewhispers us, that it 20
stands us all in hand to be forgiven as well as to
forgive. The hardest things that I know, had
their beginnings layd in the softness and yield-
ingness of a kind of dew ; and whoever would
have all men stand up stiffly for what he holds, 25
will find it best at length to lead them in those
easier paths of Nature. Sure I am, it would be
more than a wonder to me, should any ones
sight be better'd by *spitting fire* into clay & be-
smearing eyes with it. For every mans mind is
his

his Castle; and if it can't be taken by strength of reason, the throwing in Granadoes, will be nothing but a smutty, stinking token to the world, that ill will would have done more mischief, but weak Gear could not. So long as he who has but a teeming brain, may have leave to lay his eggs in his own nest, which is built beyond the reach of every mans puddering pole, why should the ears of all the neighborhood be dinn'd & grated with the Cackle, as if the whole world besides were all Weasils and Poulcats, vermine and Lurchers? I do verily bear my self in hand, that if the humor of huffing be but a little further cocker'd & more warmed, the *Leyden* gown must needs take place of the Long robe at *Cambridge* & *Oxford*, instead of the *side thing* the *thing by the side*, and snicking and sneeing will be nothing else in the world but writing of Book *a la mode d' Angleterre.* For so long as men have but unlike thinkings, and that will be as long as they have unlike faces, they must look for no better fare from a world of Bears and Scratchers, than first to be gall'd in the tenderest part of their good name, and then to fall under the rods and axes of a cutting hate, and ill will set on fire. Were I but to whisper to him of whom so many talk aloud, I should rown him thus much in the ear, with all the heartiness of a friend, that the next time he has left to bless us with his Day breaks, he would chuse a softer quill to make his pen of;

that

that the Reader at length might be as ready to
have good thoughts for him, as he has been to
have bad words for others.

As for the way of wording it, I know afore-
hand, 'tis not trim enough for these Gay days   5
of ours; but dressing is none of my business. When
I look at things, I can afford to overlook words,
and I had rather speak home than fair, nor do I
care how blunt it be, so it be strong. Every man
has *his* way of writing and speaking, and I have 10
mine; which as I allow it to others, I may look it
should be allow'd me. Only tis like there is one
thing which I may be blam'd for by many; and
that is a kind of shiness all along of those borrowed words & gaynesses, that Englishmen have 15
pickt and cull'd from other Tongues, under the
name of Choyce words and Sparkling sayings.
To which, after I have markt, how a greater
man than I, in the same business of *Bodies*, has
gone a good way towards it already, I mean the 20
Learned Sir *Kenhelm Digby*, I have but thus much
more to say, That thinking with my self, how I
an English man would write a Book in English
tongue, I made it now and then a little of my
care, to bring in so many words of that speech, 25
that the Book might thence be call'd English,
without mis-calling it. And indeed however our
smoother tongued Neighbours may put in a
claim for those bewitcheries of speech that flow
from Gloss and Chimingness; yet I verily be-
                                                    lieve

lieve that there is no tongue under heaven, that
goes beyond our English for speaking manly
strong and full. And if words be more to teach
than tickle, as I reckon they are, our Mother
tongue will get as much by speaking fit and af- 5
ter kind, as it can loose by faring rough and
taking up the tongue to utter, and more than
any else can gain by kembing better and running glibber. Besides where I thought an outlandish word would be better taken, I have 10
often for the Readers sake set it down, as for
my own sake set an English by it, as thinking
it unmeet to force my *words* upon another, in
such a piece as where I was to leave all free, as
to the *things* I spake about. Only I thought it 15
not amiss, after I was once in, for the taking off
that charge that some have too heedlesly layd
upon our speech, of a patcht up Tongue from
Lands and kinreds round about, to shew, that
a Book of thus many sheets, might be under- 20
standingly and roundly written, in hail and
clear English, without taking in from abroad,
so much as twice so many words (and he that
writes it in the most unbroken tongue upon
earth, shall go near to light upon so many), un- 25
less where the same thing is fuller and kind-
lyer spoken by those we have at home, taking
but out the Cant words or terms of art, as they
are call'd, which are rather tallies or spells in the
tongue, that is, no bodies, because every bodies,
than

than the homebred vvords of any vvhatsoever; and are taken up and forged at will, by the whole stock of learned men in all Lands, wherewith to fish out one anothers meaning. And as for a tongue that borrows not nor spends, I be- 5 lieve 'tis no where to be found, or ever will be : all tongues through time being so far blended, that there are not any of those now in the world in whole, that were at the great *Speechbreak* at *Babel*, any more than there would be 10 the same bodies crew of atoms to those Speakers now that they had then, or the same kinreds of men unmingled with Out-setters that were among them then, should they have liv'd and jugg'd together to this day. Yet that some 15 tongues lose more than others at home, and get from abroad, is easie to be seen, and our own is enough to bring any man to believe it. And in earnest, if the knack of borrowing, or robbing and pilfering rather, gets but a little further 20 ground amongst us, at the scantling it has done hitherto, it will in time to come be harder for an English-man to speak his own tongue without mingling others with it, than to speak a medly of sundry others without bringing in his own. 25 But for my part, I am of the mind, that the larding of Latine with *High-Dutch*, in what is written to the whole world, as some *Germans* in their Motley Books have already done, is even as praise-worthy, as the haling in of Latine or other

ther tongues, when we are speaking in English
to *English*; and the rather, for that the words
thus foisted in, are of such a sort most an end, that
if you look but to their rifts, and lay their beto-
kenings to the things whose names they bear, I   5
dare undertake twenty for one, that even the
slighted and off-cast words in the mouths of
Handy-crafts-men and Earth-tillers shal be better drawn and more patly brought in. And inasmuch as that *Fellowship* of *Worthies* in *London*, 10
who are now embodied under the name of *Royal*, have given us already so many new things,
and are daily starting more, neither named nor
known by those before us; and for the enriching
of the *English* tongue, as well as fulfilling of 15
Englands stores, have thought fit their discoveries should almost wholly come abroad in our
own Speech, as they are happily made in our
own Land: I think it will well become those of
us, who have a more hearty love for what is our 20
own than wanton longings after what is others,
to take light and life from such happy beginnings, and either to fetch back some of our
own words, that have been justled out in wrong
that worse from elsewhere might be hoisted in, 25
or else to call in from the fields and waters, shops
and work-housen, from the inbred stock of more
homely women and less filching Thorps-men,
that well-fraught world of words that answers
works, by which all Learners are taught to do,
and

and not to make a Clatter; And perhaps if we
slip this tide, we shall never come again at such
a nicking one.　For inasmuch as almost the
whole of those words, that we speak in things or
knowledges of things that are not body, are ta-　5
ken from things that are body, and spoken in a
borrowed meaning from thence, either as they
have Beings from God, or a Suchness of being
from our handy-work: so all the words about
body and hangers on to body that we have to　10
do with, are either such as flow from or mainly
well fall in with those that are utter'd by Work-
men, for such things as are done by hand-deed.
Now the *Philosophy* of our day and Land being
so much workful as the world knows it to be,　15
methinks this of all times should be *the* time,
wherein, if ever, we should gather up those scat-
ter'd words of ours that speak works, rather
than to suck in those of learned air from beyond
Sea, which are as far off sometimes from the　20
things they speak, as they are from us to whom
they are spoken.

　　Besides, it may well be doubted, whether
Latine can now be made so fit to set forth the
things of a *Working Philosophy* by, as our own　25
Speech, or those other of our Neighbours, who
are with us carrying on that way of *Doing*. For
we must know, that almost all the old pieces of
good Latine that we draw by, have been taken
up by that sort of learning that is wont to be
worded

worded in the Schools, & spent in the setting to
sale of such things as could best be glazed with
the froth of ink, by the men of Closets. Whence
he that is best skill'd in it, is so hard put to it, in
the Kitchin, the Shop, and the Ship; and ever will 5
be, though *Plautus* should be as well understood
as *Tully.* For the words that are every day running to and fro in the Chat of Workers, have
not been gotten into Books and put aboard for
other Lands, until this way of Knowing by Do- 10
ing was started amongst us. So that we and o-
thers of the *Handed Philosophers* may either
find better words among our own Yeomanry,
for such businesses of workmanship as are already known by name, or at least coin fitter for 15
new ones in a likewiseness to the old, than can
be lent us from that Tongue wherein we know
not how the Folks talkt in the Country, nor do
any body else or ever shall do. Whereby too we
shall not only vvith more ease and kindliness be 20
understood by the *Pains-taking* men amongst
us, whose *Crafts* will be more helpful to an
hail Philosopher, than the *Bookishness* of others.
But as Learnings being lockt up in the Tongues
of the Schools, or Love's being lickt up in the 25
more womanly simprings of the lips, and the
smiling kissing speeches of some others abroad,
have been enough to enkindle in us a panting
after, and fondness for some of those Outlandish
dynns: So if the works of our own men shall
be

be shipt over by words of our own tongue, it may happily make others who have love enough for the things, to seek as much after our words, as we upon other scores have done after theirs; the first draught being *English*, name and thing, 5 doing and speaking. Which while we forbear to do, and snip here and snatch there from some of them, being as much beholden to them for new and handsom words, as they to us for fresh and useful things, the works are not more 10 greatned by their spreading name, than the workers seem lessened by the unluckiness of the slur, That *English-men* can do by their own Hands, what they can't speak in their own Tongues.

NOTES

WHITLOCK

I have located most of Whitlock's references, but a few have proved elusive. His learning though wide is not always at first hand, and sometimes his memory, I suspect, is creative rather than accurate. In view of the projected full edition of *Zootomia* by Mr. McCrea Hazlett of Chicago University I have not felt it necessary to delay publication of this brief extract till all references were tracked down. I annotate sufficiently to show the nature of Whitlock's reading.

Page 4. l. 9. *nove dicta, etsi non nova.* St. Vincent of Lerins, *Commonitorium*, ch. 22 : ' Eadem tamen quae didicisti doce, ut cum dicas nove, non dicas nova ' (Migne, *Patrol. Lat.* l. 667). But the phrase, in the form ' non dicas nova sed nove ' is quoted by Cornelius a Lapide in his commentary on Eccl. xii. 12. See note on page 5, lines 8-9.

ll. 13-14. *Nil dictum quod non dictum prius.* Terence, *Eunuchus*, 41. Burton quotes this ' *Old Saw* ' (ed. Shilleto, i. 23), and so does Cornelius a Lapide. See note on page 5, lines 8-9.

l. 15. *various Descant on plainer Rudiments.* This recalls the Overburian definition of the Character as ' wit's descant on any plain song'.

l. 22. Juvenal, *Satires*, i. 1.

Page 5. ll. 2-4. Whitlock seems to have misread his source. Cornelius a Lapide (see note on lines 8-9 below) quotes this passage and attributes it to ' Proclus Orat. in Chrysost.' Cornelius has expanded phrases from St. Proclus's oration (Migne, *Patrol. Graeca*, lxv. 832).

ll. 8-9 and 14-15. These phrases come from Cornelius a Lapide's commentary on Eccl. xii. 12. In the same part of this commentary are to be found the passages from Terence (page 4, lines 13-14) and Seneca (lines 18-21 below) and the passage attributed to St. Chrysostome (lines 2-4 above).

ll. 18-21.   Seneca, *Ep. Mor.* xxxiii. 11.   See note on lines 8-9 above.   Vives quotes this passage in the preface to *De Disciplinis* ;   so does Jonson in his *Discoveries* ;   it is one of the bandied notions in the Ancients-Moderns controversy.

Page 6. ll. 24-30.   Persius, *Satires*, i. 41-47, omitting lines 44 and 46.

Page 7. l. 2.   *Mr. Holliday.*   His translation (*Aulus Persius Flaccus his Satires*) first appeared at Oxford in 1616.

ll. 13-15.   Cicero, *Tuscul.* i. xv. 34.

Page 8. ll. 2-7.   Pliny, *Ep.* iii. vii. 14.

ll. 25-27.   From the same essay, ' Des Livres ', as the previous quotation from Montaigne.

Page 9. ll. 2-3.   *Cancellos suæ Methodi.*   I have not found a particular source for this phrase.   Compare Bacon, *Advancement of Learning* (*Works*, ed. Ellis, Spedding, and Heath, iii. 292) and *De Aug. Sc.* (*Works*, i. 665) ; Cornwallis, in the rest of the sentence partly quoted by Whitlock on page 21, lines 11-17, says ' I professe not method, neither will I chain my selfe to the head of my Chapter'.

ll. 12 ff.   This is a constant theme of Montaigne's essay ' Des Livres ' :   ' Ie ne fois rien sans gayeté, et la continuation et contention trop ferme esblouït mon iugement, l'attriste et le lasse'.   He praises Plutarch and Seneca in particular for not demanding ' l'obligation d'un long travail'.   Whitlock's remarks here place him with the anti-Ciceronians.   For an excellent summary of this subject see F. P. Wilson, *Elizabethan and Jacobean* (1945), pp. 29 ff.

l. 21.   *Mucrones Sermonum.*   Bacon calls his *Apophthegms* ' *Mucrones Verborum*, Pointed Speeches'.

l. 26.   *Expectaltee.*   *O.E.D.* suggests a corruption of Sp. *espectante*, ' one who is on the look-out'.

ll. 29-30.   This is Bacon's objection, transferred to

the Schoolmen :   *Works,* ed. cit. iii. 286.   The origin is Quintilian, x. i. 130.

Page 10. ll. 2-3.   Seneca, *Ep. Mor.* c. 12.

ll. 9-11.   Hall, *Heaven upon Earth* (1624) :   *Works* (1625), p. 73.

l. 28.   *Nos nihil scire.*   Seneca, *Ep. Mor.* lxxxviii. 46.

Page 11. ll. 6 and 14.   *Satyra Seria* ;   *Interiora Rerum.* Bacon, *De Aug. Sc.* (*Works,* ed. cit. i. 730).   Whitlock does not quote exactly and his ' *elsewhere* ' (line 13) suggests he is quoting from memory.

ll. 9-12.   Juvenal, *Satires,* i. 30-31.

Page 12. l. 15.   G. Williamson (*P.Q.*, xv, 1936, p. 261 n. 13) mentions, as two examples of books of ' vulgar Errors ' which preceded Whitlock, Dr. James Primrose's *De Vulgi Erroribus* (1639) which was translated by Dr. Wittie in 1651, and Sir Thomas Browne's *Pseudodoxia Epidemica* (1646).

ll. 19-22.   Juvenal, *Satires,* i. 85-87.

ll. 23-27.   Stapylton published *The first six books of Juvenal* in 1644 and *Juvenal's Sixteen Satyrs* in 1647. Whitlock quotes from memory and inaccurately.

Page 13. l. 10.   *Actum agere.*   Burton (ed. cit. i. 19) quotes this phrase and refers to Terence, *Ph.* ii. iii. 70.   It is actually an adaptation of l. 72 : ' "actum" aiunt "ne agas." '

Page 14. ll. 6-8.   Seneca, *Ep. Mor.* lxxxix. 23.

l. 10.   *profitable.*   G alters to *profitables.*   *O.E.D.* cites this passage for the use of *profitable* as an adverb, but gives no other example.

ll. 20-24.   Seneca, *Ep. Mor.* viii. 6.

Page 15. ll. 3-6.   Seneca, *Nat. Quaest.* iii. 2.

ll. 13-14.   Compare Seneca's frequent references to ' drafts on Epicurus ': cf. *Ep. Mor.* xiv. 17-18 and xviii. 14.

ll. 27-28.   Martial, *Epigrams* vi. lx. 3-4.

Page 16. ll. 6-8.   The story is to be found in Diogenes Laërtius, vi. 64.

ll. 10-12.   Erasmus, *De Utilitate Colloquiorum,* ' Ad Lectorem,' first paragraph.   Erasmus wrote ' prudentiae ', not ' sapientiae '.

ll. 19-21. Petrus Servius, *Dissertatio de Unguento Armario sive de Naturæ Artisque Miraculis* (Rome, 1643), p. 179. Servius's work belongs to the same company as Kenelm Digby's discourse on the ' powder of sympathy'. A list of similar works will be found in *C.B.E.L.* i. 886 ff. Servius does not seem to have been translated into English.

l. 27. *Descants.* G alters to *Descents*, which in the sense of ' logical development ' might be correct.

Page 17. ll. 5-8. Lipsius here allies himself with the ' loose ' Senecan style. For Lipsius's importance in the history of seventeenth-century prose style see the article, ' Attic Prose : Lipsius, Montaigne, Bacon ', by Professor M. Croll in *Schelling Anniversary Papers* (1923).

ll. 14-17. Cornwallis, *Essayes*, 45, ' Of Essaies and Bookes '.

ll. 18-21. Burton quotes part of this passage (ed. cit., i. 31) with the note ' Pet. Nannius not. in Hor.', but I cannot trace it in Nannius's commentary on Horace, *De Art. Poet.*

ll. 26-28. I have not located this quotation in Vives ; he expresses similar ideas in *De Tradendis Disciplinis* II. iii, II. iv, and IV. i.

Page 18. ll. 3-4 and 8-9. These phrases are adapted from Pliny, *Hist. Nat.* xxxv. x. 80. But Whitlock no doubt had Erasmus as his immediate source : cf. the following note.

ll. 10-13. The allusion is to the Italian historian Paulus Aemilius of Verona (d. 1529) ; the passage is to be found in Erasmus, *Apophthegmata* Book VI (*Opera Omnia*, 1703, iv. 315). The same paragraph gives, more or less accurately, the passage from Pliny cited in the preceding note. I am indebted to Mr. McCrea Hazlett for this reference to Erasmus.

ll. 17-18. *Vix ea nostra voco.* Ovid, *Metam.* xiii. 141.

Page 19. l. 8. *Grammaticall.* Literal.

l. 20. *Ridentem dicere verum.* Horace, *Satires*, I. i. 24.

Page 20. ll. 3-10. *our English Bernard.* Bishop Hall. The Third Century of *Meditations and Vowes, Divine and*

Morall appeared in 1607. Whitlock's quotation is on sigs. *A*2v and *A*3.

ll. 12-13. Horace, *Ep.* II. i. 180-1.

l. 17. *momize*. To play the part of Momus ; to cavil.

l. 20. *enslaved*. It is just possible that the reading *enstaved* is correct. *O.E.D.* does not record the word ; it might be derived from the noun *stave* and mean ' bound to ', ' hooped with '.

l. 23. Although Cardinal Bellarmine died in 1621 his name was proverbial for controversy throughout the seventeenth century.

Page 21. ll. 5-6. *Expectaltees*. See note on page 9, line 26.

ll. 10-17. The ' *Ingenuous Author* ' is Cornwallis in the essay already quoted.

ll. 20-22. Strabo, *De Exordiis et Incrementis Rerum Ecclesiasticarum* (Migne, *Patrol. Lat.* cxiv. 920).

l. 26—**Page 22,** l. 4. Erasmus, *De Utilitate Collo-quiorum*, ' Ad Lectorem ', first sentence.

Page 23. ll. 1-2. *speeches in the Parliament of Parnassus, or Liberavi Animams*. Perhaps a reference to Boccalini, *Ragguagli di Parnaso*, part of which was translated as *The New-found Politicke* in 1626. Part 1, Chapter 3, shows Apollo calling a ' high *Court of Parliament* ' in which the speeches both for length and matter seem to have been pretty free. But the analogy is not very strong and the phrase ' Liberavi Animam ' is not used.

ll. 6-9. 1 Kings vi. 2-3. I have traced no reference to these verses in Donne.

Page 24. ll. 1-3. These lines are the first of a six-line verse preface to the *Enchiridion*. I have seen them only in the 1518 edition.

FAIRFAX

Most of Fairfax's peculiar usages are recorded in *O.E.D.* I note merely a representative selection.

Page 28. l. 16. *Boak*. Used indiscriminately by Fairfax for *bulk*.

48

l. 24. *limm'd.* Tear limb from limb.

Page 30. l. 25. *crotchet.* A favourite usage of Fairfax's.

Page 32. l. 8. *dote nor dare.* This particular combination is not recorded in *O.E.D.* Cf. ' dote or dream ' and ' droop and dare '. *Dare* : be dismayed.

ll. 26-27. An ' outlandish ' reminiscence of Horace, *De Art. Poet.* l. 11 ? ' Scimus, et hanc veniam petimusque damusque vicissim.'

Page 33. l. 1. *Learned men.* These include Samuel Parker, Henry More, Walter Charleton, and Thomas Hobbes.

l. 21. *frampled.* Frampold : peevish.

l. 26. *late Writer.* Most likely Samuel Parker, whose *Tentamina de Deo* (1665) Fairfax was most explicitly concerned to refute.

Page 35. l. 13. *cocker'd.* Indulged.

l. 14. *Leyden gown.* Fairfax perhaps refers to its medical associations, but the meaning is uncertain.

l. 16. *side thing.* Perhaps coined by Fairfax as a substitute for ' side robe ', i.e. ' long robe '.

thing by the side. The sword.

l. 17. *snicking and sneeing.* Fighting with knives, cut and thrust.

Page 36. l. 21. Digby's *Treatise of the Nature of Bodies* appeared first in 1644 in Paris ; London editions followed in 1658, 1665, and 1669.

Page 37. ll. 25-26. *unless where.* The sense seems to be ' *especially* where ', but the whole sentence is rambling and obscure.

Page 38. l. 15. *jugg'd.* Huddled together ; derives from *jouk,* roost.

Page 39. l. 3. *most an end.* Almost always.

ll. 10-12. The Royal Society was incorporated in 1662.

l. 28. *Thorps-men.* Villagers ; no doubt one of the words that have been 'justled out in wrong', but *O.E.D.* gives no earlier example.

Note on the text

Whitlock

Zootomia, or, Observations on the Present Manners of the English exists in two octavo impressions, one represented by the copy in the Guildhall Library (G) and the other by that in the British Museum (BM). These are identical, apart from the arrangement of prefatory material. The main differences in this material are that G has an irregular, additional leaf *A5-A5*v ('*A5*' is actually printed on the recto side)[1] which gives a note, 'The Publisher to the Reader', signed 'J.B.' and not in BM; and that G prints on A6-A6v a version of the opening of the preface different from that in BM. These two leaves in G present the customary theme of the careless author and the importunate friends; BM necessarily omits the note from 'J.B.' since it rewrites the opening of the preface in a firmer tone, refusing to make the conventional apologies and asserting that the work 'ventured willingly into the *World*'. It seems most likely that BM is the later impression, representing an increased vigour on Whitlock's part. I reprint from BM; the material reprinted collates A6-a8v. G has ink additions which may be in Whitlock's hand; these identify 'J.B.' as Birkenhead (the addition is : 'M : Art. alias Aulicus') and add to the commendatory poem the name 'M : Lluellin : M.D.' This copy is also emended throughout, mostly by this same hand; I have incorporated these emendations where they seemed absolutely necessary; all those suggested for the preface are noted with the list of textual changes. Mr. Williamson refers to another edition of 1664 'under the title, *Observations on the Present Manners of the English*'

---

[1]The copy in Edinburgh University Library, which is the only other copy I have seen, is the same as G except that it includes the first leaves missing from the latter. It also shows clearly that the additional leaf *A5-A5*v conjugates with the leaf A6-A6v. Mr. McCrea Hazlett will be dealing in his edition of the full work with a curious version of G which he has found in U.S. libraries.

which he has not seen and which he thinks may be 'merely the second issue with a new title-page' (*P.Q.*, xv, 1936, p. 255). I have been unable to find any other reference to this—or to a copy 'with new title-page 1679' referred to in Allibone's *Critical Dictionary* (1871).

Fairfax

No textual problem arises. The work exists, so far as I know, in only one octavo impression. The material reprinted is from the copy in the British Museum and forms the whole of the gathering sig. b.

Both prefaces are given in a page-by-page, line-by-line reprint.

Changes made in the text

Whitlock

PAGE	LINE	
8	18	*I ;] I
9	30	Verborum] erborum
12	15	*Errores] Errores,
13	5	Dramatick ;] Dramatick,
14	5	commendation] commendations
17	5	*Epistles*] *Epistlse*
20	2	*with,*] *with.*
20	3	*Bernard for,*] Bernard ; *for*
20	14	I'le] I le
20	20	enslaved] enstaved
23	27	Christiani] Chistiani

Corrections marked * have the support of ink emendations in the Guildhall copy. (The correction to Page 20, line 3 is that given in the margin of the Guildhall copy ; the text itself is made to read 'Bernard *for* ;'.) Other suggested emendations which have *not* been incorporated in the text are as follows :

PAGE	LINE	
8	18	difficult, *for* difficult ;
14	10	*profitables for profitable*
16	27	Descents *for* Descants
17	10	(*not* Pumping for ;) *for not* Pumping for ;
21	17	*me. for me*
21	18	*them, for them.*
23	10-11	Prefaces *a for* Prefaces

Fairfax

PAGE	LINE	
28	17	I e'en] I'een
30	3	which, the] which the
36	16	cull'd] cull d
36	26	call'd] call d

Two running titles have been made to conform; in the original text they are: *To the Reador.* (sig. b2v) and *To the Read.* (sig. b3).

Long ſ is replaced by s throughout both prefaces.

Pagination has been added and the original signatures have been ignored. The decoration on p. 3 and the decorated initial on p. 27 are not those of the original.